Facebook Marketing and Advertising:

The Ultimate Guide for Beginners and Startups

Table of Contents

Introduction 4

Chapter 1: Ad Campaign Structure – How to Structure Your Marketing for Optimal Results 6

Chapter 2: Who Are You Trying To Reach? – How Facebook Can Help You Find Your Audience 13

Chapter 3: How Will You Get Their Attention – Using the Right Ads for the Right Devices 20

Chapter 4: How Are Your Ads Performing? – Find Out How Your Marketing Is Driving Your Business 26

Chapter 5: What Will It Cost? – Effective Budgeting For Your Facebook Campaign 34

Conclusion 40

© Copyright 2018 by David Clarke - All rights reserved.

The following book is reproduced below with the goal of providing information that is as accurate and reliable as possible. Regardless, purchasing this book can be seen as consent to the fact that both the publisher and the author of this book are in no way experts on the topics discussed within and that any recommendations or suggestions that are made herein are for entertainment purposes only. Professionals should be consulted as needed prior to undertaking any of the action endorsed herein.

This declaration is deemed fair and valid by both the American Bar Association and the Committee of Publishers Association and is legally binding throughout the United States.

Furthermore, the transmission, duplication or reproduction of any of the following work including specific information will be considered an illegal act irrespective of if it is done electronically or in print. This extends to creating a secondary or tertiary copy of the work or a recorded copy and is only allowed with an expressed written consent from the Publisher. All additional right reserved.

The information in the following pages is broadly considered to be a truthful and accurate account of facts and as such any inattention, use or misuse of the information in question by the reader will render any resulting actions solely under their purview. There are no scenarios in which the publisher or the original author of this work can be in any fashion deemed liable for any hardship or damages that may befall them after undertaking information described herein.

Additionally, the information in the following pages is intended only for informational purposes and should thus be thought of as universal. As befitting its nature, it is presented without assurance regarding its prolonged validity or interim quality. Trademarks that are mentioned are done without written consent and can in no way be considered an endorsement from the trademark holder.

The author and publisher are in no way associated with the social media company Facebook.

Introduction

Congratulations on purchasing *Facebook Marketing and Advertising: The Ultimate Guide for Beginners and Startups*. We appreciate your interest, and we hope you find this book to be interesting, informative and helpful.

The following chapters will discuss:
- Advertisement campaign structures through the Facebook platform;
- How to target the ideal audience;
- How to create eye-catching advertisements;
- How to track the performance of your advertising campaigns;
- How to set, manage and maintain your advertising budget;
- And how to utilize the various reports within Facebook Ads Manager to ensure that your ad campaign is as successful as possible.

We will even discuss how the Facebook Ads Manager chooses which ads are shown to which consumer, whether those ads are shown in the desktop News Feed or the mobile a News Feed, the importance of copyright laws in ad design, and which software programs you may want to invest in if you want to utilize the many different reports available with Facebook Ads Manager.

We are determined to make sure that your Facebook advertising experience is positive, effective, and profitable, and that what we teach you here will only serve to benefit your business.

There are plenty of books on this subject on the market, and we are thrilled by your interest in this one! Every effort was made to ensure it is full of as much useful information as possible. Please enjoy!

Chapter 1: Ad Campaign Structure – How to Structure Your Marketing for Optimal Results

The proper ad campaign structure is crucial for any business, small or large, and any brand, whether that brand supports a single product or many products. With a well-formed, thoughtfully-designed ad campaign, your company could see an increase in website or social media traffic, an increase in profits, improved brand recognition, and so much more! An effective campaign structure is the first step in a successful ad campaign, as it will help you to set specific goals for specific campaigns, measure the results of those campaigns, discover which campaigns are working and which are not, and allocate your budget in the most effective way possible. It will also help you to create multiple ad sets for multiple audiences so that you can determine who is most likely to generate business for your company or brand. Through variations in image, text, links, and videos, a properly structured campaign will even allow you to see what types of ads are having the biggest impact on your audience.

A Facebook ad campaign has three levels. At the top is the Campaign, then the Ad Set, and then the Ad itself. At the campaign level, you will choose an objective or goal like "Increase Sales" or "Increase Total Likes for my Business Facebook Page." At the Ad Set level, you will set your budget, your schedule, your target audience, and your ad placement. Once you have chosen the parameters of your ad set, you will design your ad or multiple ads to be run with the same ad set. Your ad set may contain one or more ads, and the ads must be individual creations that contain text, video, images, and/or links. Your ad set is what will attract attention to your business or brand and will help you achieve both your short-term and long-term goals.

STEP ONE:

The first step towards creating an effective ad campaign structure is to set firm and clear goals, and then to allocate each goal to an individual campaign. Then, every ad set and ad will be oriented towards your chosen objectives - no matter how big or small, how long-term or how short term. For example, your objective may be something like increasing the number of installs your app has, increasing overall traffic to your website, increasing sales of a particular item, or simply to generate more "Likes" for your Facebook business page.

Tip #1: Limit one objective per advertisement, that way you can tailor your audience and budget to achieve maximum value from your ad campaign.

Tip #2: Get creative! If your objective is to increase Page Likes, consider designing an ad that offers a 10% discount code to anyone who Likes and Follows your business Facebook page. While this would work well for increasing Facebook Page Likes, offering 10% off for a Facebook Like may not generate more website traffic, since your website is not directly involved. This is why we recommend limiting your objectives to one objective per ad.

STEP TWO:

The second step is to allocate your ad sets to the audiences you most want to target. One ad set might be aimed at Men, age 18 to 24, while another ad set might aim at Women, age 18 to 24. It is important to allocate different ad sets to different audiences so that your ad sets do not end up competing with one other. It also important to keep your target audience in mind when designing each ad set. Men may be more likely to stop and look at an ad that includes a scantily-clad model in it, but most women will probably scroll right past - or worse, they may block the ad.

When you allocate your audience, you will also be at the point in ad set design where you will get to determine how to allocate your budget and the different aspects of budgeting you will need to keep in mind. The first two aspects of budgeting to consider are Daily Budget and Lifetime Budget.

- *Daily Budget:* the amount you are willing to spend on an ad set per day.
- *Lifetime Budget:* the amount you are willing to spend on an ad set in total.

Once your budget has been set, the Facebook Ads Manager will spread your Lifetime Budget out over the entire length of your ad campaign. Doing so may cause your Daily Budget to decrease, but Facebook Ads Manager will never exceed the Daily Budget you originally set. This ensures you that Facebook Ads Manager never goes "over-budget" on any aspect of your campaign and that you never spend more money than you are willing to spend on an ad campaign.

Tip: Set a cap on your expenditures, track how much money you have spent using Facebook's spend meters, and measure your campaign's performance using the ads reporting tab in the Facebook Ads Manager.

Tip: Avoid changing your budget type mid-campaign. Doing so will reset your budget, and this may alter the ad analysis provided by Facebook Ads manager. Also, you can use the Audience Insight feature in Ads Manager to help with your target selection.

STEP THREE:

The third step is to bid for your various objectives. For example, let us say that your chosen objective was to direct traffic to your website. In that case, Facebook Ads Manager will charge you when your ad is delivered to an audience that is most likely to click the provided link, which will then direct them to your website. You will not be charged when the link is clicked, but you will be charged each time the ad is shown to someone who has a proven history of following the links provided in advertisements. This is important because it prevents you from being charged if the same person clicks on your link repeatedly, which can happen by mistake or as a result of a malicious intent to abuse and misuse your ad campaign.

At this stage, you will also choose where you would like your ad to be placed on the Facebook platform. Ads may be displayed in the desktop News Feed, the mobile News Feed, or in the column to the right (outside of the News Feed). Displaying your ad in the column to right could be beneficial, as those ads are typically stationary and do not scroll away as the user scrolls up and down through their News Feed. Advertising in that right-hand column can generate more attention, or more consistent attention, from Facebook users. On the other hand - displaying your ad here may not provide greater attention, as many Facebook users rarely let their eyes divert away from their actual News Feed. There is no guarantee, so you may want to try a different ad campaign in each location, just to see what will work best for your ad sets and your business.

When choosing your ad location, take your demographics and target audience into serious consideration.

For example - should an ad be shown in the desktop News Feed or the mobile News Feed if the target audience is between 18 and 24 years of age? It should probably appear in the mobile News Feed, as this age group is much more likely to access Facebook on their mobile phones than on an actual computer.

Or - should an ad be shown in the desktop News Feed or the mobile News Feed if the target audience is between 65 and 80 years of age? It should probably appear in the desktop News Feed, as this age group probably does not access Facebook on their mobile phones, and if they do, they may find it difficult to read or interact with your ad set on such a small screen.

Tip: Choose multiple placement options to give your ads the best chance of engagement.

Tip: If you believe that one ad set is performing better than another, change just one of the ad settings, like: bidding, budget, placement, or targeting. Keep all other settings the same. This will reveal which setting is having the most impact, allowing you to learn more about the demographics connected to your business brand, what works, and what does not work.

STEP FOUR:

The fourth step is to create a variety of ads and see which of those ads work best for your goals. You can use a combination of text, links, images, and video, and you can use up to fifty different ads in any given ad set. If one ad, in particular, is performing poorly, you can easily turn that ad off without altering or stopping the rest of your ad campaign, and without upsetting your budget. Best of all - Facebook Ads Manager never charges you for stopping or altering your ad campaign.

Keep in mind that your ads need to be eye-catching, otherwise audience members will scroll right past them without ever looking at what you have to present.

- *Video Ads:* keep the video short and make sure any audio attached to the video is neither too loud nor too quiet. Studies show that most people will click away from any ad video that lasts longer than twenty seconds.
- *Image Ads:* keep the images small enough to display nicely on a cell phone screen, and try to include some text on or around the image. Without the text, many audience members may be unsure of what it is you are advertising or what your objective is.

Another important thing to keep in mind when designing your ads is copyright laws. Be extremely careful with the images and videos that you use. Take advantage of websites like Shutterstock.com, whether you can safely purchase images or videos that are relevant to your product, brand, or company. Or, better yet, take the photos or film the videos yourself!

If your ad includes an image or video that you found via a quick Google search, and you did not obtain the appropriate copyright release, the owner of that image or video could allege theft, could send a "Cease & Desist" letter that would require you to stop using the image or video, and could even sue you and collect some of the profits that you saw as a result of the ad campaign their image or video was used in. Copyright laws are surprisingly strict, and if there is a copyright dispute, it can be a very stressful and costly situation.

Similar to copyright laws are "intellectual property laws," which are what protect writers from plagiarism. Be careful with what you write in your ad copy. You will want to make sure the text is original. You can do this by using various plagiarism checkers that are free to use online, like www.edubirdie.com.

STEP FIVE:

Once your ad set has been published, it is very important to pay attention to ad performance. Some ads may perform better than others, and you will need to find out why one ad performs better than others, that way you can adjust your ad set (and future ad sets) accordingly.

Facebook Ads Manager allows you to turn a particular ad off if you need to. You can also cancel your ad campaign altogether. In addition, if the parameters you set for your campaign are not generating any results, Facebook Ads Manager may waive the expense of the campaign, or reimburse you if they have already collected payment.

Keep in mind that Facebook Ads Manager only bills you once a month, and only bills you for what has been spent on your ad campaign. Therefore - if you set a lifetime budget of $500 for your ad campaign, but only $25 of that $500 is spent in the month of January, then Facebook Ads Manager will only collect the $25 spent in January. This type of pay-as-you-go billing is incredibly useful for small business and those with small advertising budgets. Billing can be set up on an auto-pay schedule, using any major card. The auto-pay schedule can be customized so that you can even choose the day of the month that your payment is automatically withdrawn from your bank account or charged to your selected credit card.

Tip: *It is better to turn off an ad or ad set as opposed to completely deleting them. Deleting an ad or ad set is irreversible. Turning an ad or ad set off is like hitting that pause button. This way you can turn them back on later, if necessary, and after you have adjusted whatever parameter was preventing your ad from performing well. You can also turn the ad set off if you suddenly find that you need to make an emergency change to your advertising budget.*

Chapter 2: Who Are You Trying To Reach? – How Facebook Can Help You Find Your Audience

Facebook provides a number of ways to attract people to your business. Through a combination of demographics, pre-existing data on your current customer base, and ways of finding people similar to those who have stimulated your business in the past, Facebook can help you build your audience. Facebook Ads Manager separates the different types of audience into three categories: Core Audiences, Custom Audiences, and Lookalike Audiences.

I.   Core Audiences

Facebook Ads Manager allows you to manually narrow down your Core Audience by the following factors:

- **Location:** There are four options which shape the scope of your audience targeting.
    - Everyone (for everyone in a given area)
    - Locals (those that claim the area as "home")
    - New Residents (those who have recently updated the area as "home")
    - Visitors (those have recently "checked in" to this location, or nearby locations)

    The "given area" can be the narrowed down by your zip code, and can even include neighboring zip codes if you are looking for a broader reach. The location of your audience is important to consider, as not every business is looking for tourists and not every business is looking for locals.

- *For example*: a hotel would want to target visitors and tourists, whereas a bakery will want to target local residents.

Consider location carefully before making a decision about which locations or areas to include in your campaign. If you are advertising a product that can be shipped outside of your state, or outside of your country, then you will want the location to be very broad. However, if you are advertising a specific service, you may only want to advertise in the area that you are willing to provide this service.

- *For example:* If your business is a Maid service, you may only want to advertise within the sixty square miles of your home or business. It probably would not make sense to advertise your Maid service hundreds of miles away.

- **Demographics:** Facebook allows marketers to target specific age ranges, specific genders, and specific spoken languages.

    - *Age Ranges:* while a hotel would want to target all age ranges, a tattoo parlor may only want to target people under the age of 40. Be sure to choose an age range that suits your product or business.

    - *Genders:* again, while a hotel may want to target all genders, a hair salon may only want to target women. 90% of the time, you will want to target both men and women, so consider very carefully before choosing to exclude either gender.

- *Languages:* if the staff at your business speak more than language, it is important to advertise this. For example, if your business is based in Southwest Arizona, and you (or a staff member) are fluent in Spanish, as well as English, advertise to both English-speaking and Spanish-speaking customers.

- **Interest:** Targeting by interest allows marketers to reach people based on what they have listed as their interests and activities on their Facebook profile, the posts and comments that they have "liked" on Facebook, and the posts and comments that they have created. For example, if your business makes customized dog collars, Facebook Ads Manager will target users who have dogs, follow dog- or pet-related pages, or have dogs listed as an interest in their profile.

- **Behavior:** Targeting by behavior allows marketers to reach people based on what they buy, what kinds of devices they use, whether they are using a desktop to access Facebook or a mobile phone, and other similar factors. For example, if you are advertising your new iPhone app, Facebook Ads Manager will target users who access Facebook via their iPhone or other Apple-branded product. After all, iPhone apps are only available for iPhones and cannot be used across other mobile phone platforms or operating systems.

- **Connections:** Targeting by connections allows marketers to select their audience based on their connections to pages, apps, or events. It also allows you to target the friends of people connected to pages and apps.

- Example: if your business is a bakery, you can target audience members that have liked other bakeries in your area.
- Example: if your business is a tattoo parlor, you can target audience members that have liked Facebook pages related to tattoos.

- **Audience size:** Be aware that with every factor you use to narrow your audience, your target audience may become very small. This is where it is important to consider including zip codes beyond your own. Be sure to pay close attention to the Audience Size Indicator provided by the Facebook Ads Manager, to make sure you are not spending a large amount of your budget on a very small or narrow audience.

II. Custom Audiences

Custom Audiences are audiences built on your own data, as opposed to the Core Audiences which are based solely on Facebook's data. Custom Audience sources can come from data files (from your Point of Sale system, your email lists, or your client database). Custom Audience sources can also come from website data (data collected from your company's website), mobile app data (data collected from your company's mobile apps), or Facebook data (data collected from people's interactions with your Facebook page, ads, and videos).

Make sure your data sources coincide with your goals. For example, if you are looking to drive up sales and increase revenue, you should be targeting frequent shoppers and high-value clients.

It is also important to ensure that the proper devices have been targeted. For instance, if your audience tends to shop more via mobile phone, your targeting should reflect this. Use complete and up-to-date data for the best results.

Tip: If you are using an email list to generate your audience, make sure that email list is up-to-date, and not riddled with old email accounts that are no longer in use. Using old information will only result in your ad budget being wasted.

You can also use your Custom Audience data to target customers based on their previous interactions with your business.

- If a customer has made a prior purchase, you could advertise complementary products.
- Re-market old products to members of your audience that have already encountered your message.
- Use Custom Audiences to upsell.
- Use Custom Audiences to show new customers that they have friends or connections that like your business or use your product or service.

A note on security: Facebook uses a security process called "data hashing," which heavily encrypts your data. Facebook's data hashing has been reviewed by an independent third party, PricewaterhouseCoopers, and they have confirmed that your data is secure - from the implementation of your data to the storage of your data. So, you need not worry that the audience information you share or the payment information you provide is vulnerable to cyber threats. While no system can ever be 100% secure, Facebook's data hashing severely limits the actual threat to your information.

III. Lookalike Audiences

Lookalike Audiences are people who have similar online traits to your current customer base. There are three types of Lookalike Audiences: Value-Based Lookalikes, International Lookalikes, and Multi-Country Lookalikes.

- **Value-Based Lookalikes**: When creating a Custom Audience, you can create a customer value file which will help you find new customers who are similar to your highest spending, or high-value, clients. For example, if many of your high-value clients are considered "upper class," you may want to target an audience that frequents expensive local restaurants or local golf clubs. When creating a Value-Based Lookalike audience in Facebook Ads Manager, it is important that stereotypes exist for a reason, and stereotypes can definitely be used to your advantage in terms of marketing and advertising.
- **International Lookalikes:** For a company to expand across the globe, Lookalike Audiences can target those who most resemble your customer base in any country - not just in one particular region. This is especially valuable if your company provides goods with international shipping options.
- **Multi-Country Lookalikes:** Target a region, such as Europe or North America, and market across multiple countries at the same time. This is especially valuable if your business is located near another country. For example, if your business is located in northern Michigan, targeting audience members in Canada may be beneficial, as they may be willing to cross the border if your services are of particular interest to them.

To create a Lookalike Audience, you must first create a Seed Audience. This is a sample of at least one hundred of your best customers - those that are heavily engaged in your online content, or those who make the largest or most valuable purchases. The more people in your Seed Audience, the better Facebook can help find Lookalike audiences.

Seed Audiences can be created from Custom Audiences, from data collected from your website and/or mobile app, and from the data collected from your Facebook pages. When creating a Lookalike Audience, it is important to consider your end goal. Are you looking for a new audience similar to your existing audience? Or are you looking to broaden your overall reach by adding to your existing audience?

When choosing your audience size in the Facebook Ads Manager, know that if your audience size is closer to "one," you will get a smaller but more similar audience to your current seed audience. If the audience size number in the Facebook Ads Manager is closer to "ten," you will get a larger, broader audience, but it may contain fewer (if any) similarities to that of your seed audience.

A final note on Audiences: Once you have saved your Core Audience, Custom Audience, and Lookalike Audience, you can access them for future ad campaigns in the Facebook Ads Manager. You can also alter their parameters in the event that overlap between your various audiences lowers the delivery of your ad sets.

If you have multiple ad sets targeting similar audiences during the same period of time, then your ad sets might end up competing with each other in the ad auction. This can drive up prices and lead to an inefficient or ineffective use of your budget.

Chapter 3: How Will You Get Their Attention – Using the Right Ads for the Right Devices

The following chapter will discuss the various types of ads that you can create for your Facebook marketing campaign, including photo ads, video ads, messenger ads, carousel ads, slideshow ads, and collection ads.

I. Photo Ads

Using images is an excellent way to promote your work, your business, and/or your brand. It has been proven that using images online is much more effective in getting the attention of your audience than text copy ads alone.

Facebook photo ads are simple and straightforward. With the right image and accompanying text copy, people are much more likely to notice your brand. Photos are also excellent for increasing your audience's awareness of your products and/or services. People are much more likely to buy a product if they can see it first.

Consider using photo ads for any new products that your business is promoting. Photo ads are also very easy to make. You can simply add a photo to a page post, giving that post an automatic little boost. Photo ads work great for both desktop and mobile devices.

As always, make sure the images you are using are either free of copyright or that you own the copyright or copyright release to them.

II. Video Ads

Facebook understands that people want different kinds of videos in different situations. For instance, if someone is on their mobile device, they are probably on-the-go and would prefer to watch something short. Meanwhile, if a person is on a larger device (like a laptop) and sitting on the couch, then they are likely more willing to watching a longer video.

For shorter videos, you might want to consider using in-feed ads. Whether your goal is to reinforce your brand or promote a new product, in-feed ads capitalize on quick, short spurts of attention from your target audience to promote your business.

Create a captivating video which quickly tells your story, and people, while scrolling through their feed, will stop to hear what your company has to say. Using video ads is a great way to drive sales. Furthermore, by combining video ads with product images and carousels, you can stimulate the interest of your audience and potentially increase your sales.

You can also create video ads that appear "in-stream," meaning the ad is shown after the viewer has begun watching a video. In-stream video ads can be as long as fifteen seconds, but the shorter they are, the better. Research shows that 70% of in-stream ads are watched to completion, with the audio/sound on. This allows you to deliver a more dynamic message to your audience.

Another advantage to using video ads on Facebook is that it allows your company to reach people that you might not otherwise reach with more expensive television ads. Research shows that Facebook video ads reach 37% percent more people in the age group of 18 to 24. Facebook is also creating new ways of using video to engage your audience. With Facebook 360 your customers can interact with the video to explore a 3D or panoramic environment. This is particularly useful for businesses like Real Estate Agencies - instead of posting a picture of a house, they can create a 3D or panoramic video of the interior of the house. This is much more eye-catching and attention-getting than a simple picture!

Finally, using Facebook Creative Hub, you can create "mock-up" or tester video ads, and then test them in real time. This allows you to see how various types of video ads may affect your audience and allows you to view these video ads from the perspective of your audience. This is especially important if you are interested in running a video ad in the News Feed of mobile phones, as the Mobile-view can restrict what appears on the screen.

As always, make sure the images you are using are either free of copyright or that you own the copyright or copyright release to them.

III. Messenger Ads

Messenger ads are ads that appear in Facebook Messenger, as opposed to the News Feed of your audience members. Research shows that 2 billion Facebook messages pass between people and businesses each month. Using Messenger in this way is an incredibly effective way to engage current customers and to attract a wealth of new customers.

The best way to use Facebook Messenger, and to capitalize on its worldwide reach, is to place your ads on the Facebook Messenger home screen. This way, ads are mixed in with your customer list of conversations and are therefore difficult to ignore.

Messenger ads work in the same way that other ads do across the Facebook platform. Ads appear where they are most likely to boost your campaign, at the lowest possible cost to you. When your customers tap on the ads appearing on their home screen, they will automatically and immediately be sent to whichever destination you selected during the creation of the ad, such as your website, your app, the product page you created, or a dialogue with your company on Facebook Messenger.

Using Facebook Messenger to promote your business has three essential advantages:

- You can start new conversations by using Facebook Messenger ads, which allows you to open a direct dialogue between your business or brand and the potential new or repeat customer.

- You can stay on top of Facebook Messenger conversations with existing or return customers by utilizing Facebook Messengers high-level view of existing or open conversations.

- You can re-initiate old conversations with customers that you have not interacted with or touched base with after a certain period of time.

IV. Carousel Ads

Carousel ads allow you to use multiple images within a single ad. Each image can have its own link, and you can also use videos. Carousel ads allow you to showcase multiple products, various aspects of a single product or service, current promotions, or even convey a story about your company or brand that unfolds across each carousel card.

This ad format is dynamic and can be used to reach any number of your company's marketing goals. Carousel ads have a number of advantages over other types. Carousel ads give marketers a lot more space to be creative and engaging within the ten carousel cards available. They are also highly-interactive, allowing you to link to multiple websites or product pages. Your audience can also swipe or click on your carousel cards to move the story along, or visit whatever page you have linked to the image or video in question. And finally, because you have ten cards to fill with video or imagery, you have the flexibility to tell your story or feature your products in new and creative ways.

Whether you are showcasing multiple products, highlighting the various features of a single product, telling a story, or explaining a process, Carousel ads are a flexible and dynamic way to promote your business or brand.

V. Slideshow Ads

A Slideshow ad is like a video ad. It uses images, motion, text, and sound - all to tell a compelling or dynamic story. Slideshow ads work on any device and typically are not limited by slow internet or data speeds, the way some video ads are.

You can create a slideshow ad easily and quickly, whether for desktop or mobile devices, and you can use that slideshow to tell the story of your company, describe your product, or showcase a new line of products. You can use stock images made available by Facebook in the ad creation process, or even use existing video footage.

Slideshows are captivating, much like video ads are, but they are easier to create, less expensive to run, and less time consuming to maintain. They also tend to run more easily and more smoothly across all devices - from desktop to mobile, and everything in between.

As always, make sure the images you are using are either free of copyright or that you own the copyright or copyright release to them.

Tip: *Consider using a Slideshow Ad to determine what your audience may find compelling as a Video Ad. Slideshow Ads can be valuable "test runs" before you spend your time or money to create a Video Ad that may not generate the attention you had hoped for or planned on. Slideshow Ads are fast and easy to create and require very little planning on your part.*

VI. Collection Ads

Using a combination of video and imagery, Facebook Collection Ads are a great way to sell products, particularly via mobile phone. Because people are spending so much more time on their phones, and because this is changing the way they search, learn, and buy, Collections Ads are an ideal way to adapt to these changing circumstances. Your customers expect fast-loading, engaging, smooth video mobile experiences, so once a customer has tapped your ad, they can learn more about the features of your products seamlessly.

This ad format is seamless, and almost guaranteed to generate new business. Many Collections Ads include a video at the top of the ad, with a slideshow of images beneath the video - all of which are clickable and can provide your audience with direct access to your website, your product pages, and more. These ads are ideal for mobile devices because they tend to take up the entire screen of the mobile device - guaranteeing that the audience member viewing the ad is not distracted by any other content within their Facebook feed. You have their complete and undivided attention until they scroll away from the ad.

As always, make sure the images you are using are either free of copyright or that you own the copyright or copyright release to them.

Tip: *To make sure your Collections Ad is full of strong, effective content, consider trying the different aspect of the ad individually first. Post a Slideshow Ad with the images and test how well your audience responds to that Slideshow before including it in your Collections Ad. Furthermore, run a Video Ad alone as a test, before including it in your Collection Ad. This will guarantee that your Collections Ad is as effective as possible and that it will generate the response you have been looking for.*

Chapter 4: How Are Your Ads Performing? – Find Out How Your Marketing Is Driving Your Business

Once your campaign has begun and you are delivering ads to your pre-selected target audience, you need to know whether or not those ads are having the impact you are seeking on the audience you selected, and *why* they are having that impact.

You need to know:

- The demographics you are reaching.
- The types of devices that have been used to view your ad.
- How many unique people you have reached across various platforms.

With people-based metrics across multiple platforms, Facebook Ads Manager can help businesses fill in these blanks. All of this information is easily accessible within the Facebook Ads Manager, allowing you to tailor your ads to your needs, to your audience, and to your budget. This is a highly customizable experience, and the simple, easy-to-use interface makes the Facebook Ads Manager ideal for those without experience advertising, and those trying to start or grow a new business.

With the Ad Performance tools built into the Facebook Ads Manager, you can quickly learn which ads your audience prefers, which products or services they are most interested, and who your true target demographic is. Facebook Ads Manager will give you every tool you need to successfully market your business, brand or product, all on your own!

I. Ads Manager Overview

The following is a list of terms you will need to know to use Ads Manager effectively:

- **Delivery:** This refers to your ad campaigns, ad sets, and ads and their overall status. This determines how your ad is seen by your target audience.

- **Results:** This refers to the objectives you defined when you initially set up your ad campaign. For example, if you selected Page Views as your objective, the Results column will show you how many times your page has been viewed.

- **Reach vs. Impressions:** Reach is the number of people who have seen your ad at least once. Reach is different from "Impressions," in that Impressions include people who have seen your ad multiple times. They refer to those audience members as "Impressions," because your ad obviously left an impression on them for them to view it more than once.

- **Cost per Results:** This is the average amount your ad costs per result. It is calculated by dividing the amount spent by the amount in the Results column. For example, if your company spent $100 on a conversion campaign, and your ad netted 50 conversions, then the cost per result would amount to $2. Therefore, you paid $2 for each view your ad received.

- **Amount Spent:** This is the total amount your company has spent on ads, ad sets, and campaigns. It always shows the last 30 days by default. As mentioned previously, Facebook Ads Manager bills you on a monthly basis - you do not have to pay for the entire ad campaign at once. This is incredibly beneficial to those with small budgets or those that are new to advertising, that may need to adjust their budgets as time goes on.

- **Ends:** This is the date your campaign is scheduled to end. This date is chosen when the ad campaign is initially scheduled and published. This end date is not set in stone, however, and you can add time to any ad campaign that you want with a few simple clicks. However - keep in mind that extending your campaign will alter you budget. If you do not increase your budget at the same time that you extend your ad campaign, then less of your budget will be spent per day, to make up for that extension. Extending an ad campaign is only wise if you can increase your budget, as well.

II. *How to use Reporting Controls within Facebook Ads Manager*

Reporting controls are used to locate specific campaigns, to find out which ads are performing well, and which ones need to be turned off or altered. You can use the following options to find the information that you may be looking for:

- Search
    - This will allow you to customize a report based on keywords and responses. This is especially helpful if you are trying to locate a specific reaction(s) from your audience. Try organizing your report by searching for keywords like: love, great, awesome.
    - You can also use negative keywords to identify campaigns that are having a less positive response. Try organizing your report by searching for keywords like: expensive, scam, poor.

- Date Range
    - This will allow you to arrange a report that details your ad campaigns in any date range that you choose. This can help you identify trends that your business may experience with advertising - if there are certain months that are busier or more profitable than others.
- Breakdown
    - The breakdown feature gives you an incredibly detailed report and a wealth of information. You may want to use this report control in conjunction with the report filters, that way you are not overwhelmed with information.
- Filters
    - These filters make the Facebook reports exceptionally customizable, allowing you to remove or add any data field that you want to create a report that will detail exactly what you need to know.
- Columns
    - You can arrange these columns in whatever organizational method you choose - especially if you intend to export your reports to Microsoft Excel.

Using these parameters can help you identify which demographics are most successful if there was a certain period of time that your ad campaign saw the most traction. Study these reports closely; there is no limit to what you can learn about your ad campaign from them!

Tip #1: If you do not have Microsoft Excel, you can purchase it online as part of the Microsoft Office Suite, directly from Microsoft. This suite of programs typically includes Microsoft Office and more, and is updated on a yearly basis - so you may need to purchase the new version each year. Visit www.microsoft.com/office/store for details, pricing and more.

Tip #2: *You can also use Google Sheets in lieu of Microsoft Excel, and best of all, Google Sheets is completely **free** - all you need is an active Gmail account! Google also offers free office software like Google Docs (similar to Microsoft Office, Google Slides (similar to Microsoft PowerPoint), and Google Forms (a .pdf creator). For more information on Google Sheets, visit www.google.com/sheets/about/.*

Tip #3: *If you do not have access to the Microsoft Office Suite, and you do not have an active Gmail account for the Google line of office software products, you can download OpenOffice. This program is 100% free and is both easy to install and easy to use. It is designed to serve all of the same functions as the Microsoft Office Suite but without the expense. The OpenOffice equivalent of Microsoft Excel is OpenOffice Calc. The program is supported entirely through donations, so if you can, consider donating to Open Office if you like their suite of programs. For more information, visit www.openoffice.org/sc/*

III. Analyzing your Results

The following list will help you to understand the significance of the various results you may find in the Facebook Ads Manager report generator.

- **Brand Awareness:** This provides an estimation as to the number of people who may remember your ads within a two-day period. This result is significant if you have objectives such as Video Views, Engagement, Brand Awareness, and Post Engagement. The reason they chose to a two day period is simply that studies show that if you recall seeing an ad two days after you initially saw it, you are significantly more likely to recall the name of the product or business a week or even a month later.

- **Reach vs. Impressions:** Reach is the number of people who have seen your ad at least one time. Reach is different from Impressions in that Impressions include people who have seen your ad multiple times, whether because they seek it out repeatedly or because it appears in their News Feed repeatedly.

- **Traffic:** This provides the number of actions your ads have contributed to your mobile app, and therefore recorded as "app events." This also provides the number of clicks your ads have received on desktop and mobile devices, which allows you to track how many people have used your ad to access your website - or whatever other clickable content has been attached.

- **Engagement:** This provides the total number of actions your ads have stimulated. This includes Facebook page "Likes" from ad engagement, the number of people that marked themselves as "Interested" or "Going To" an event your company has organized and streaming reactions from live broadcasts. This information is vital when determining whether or not your ad campaign has been successful.

- **App Installs:** This provides the total number of "app events." By "app events," we are referring to the installation of your app or the uninstallation of your app. This records how effectively your ads are contributing to the success of your mobile application.

- **Video Views:** This provides the number of views your video ads have received. The view is only counted if it has lasted for an aggregate of three seconds or more. It also indicates how many times your videos have been watched to completion.

- **Lead Generation:** This provides the number of forms your customers have filled out online, as a result of Facebook lead ads.

- **Messages:** This provides the number of Facebook Messenger messages exchanged between your company and your customers.

- **Conversions:** Conversions are chosen at the ad set level. This may include "Add to Cart," "Initiate Checkout," and "Make Purchase," if your goal is to obtain direct product sales from your ad campaign.

- **Catalog Sales:** This provides the number of sales recorded at your stores as a result of Facebook ads, as recorded by Facebook Pixel.

- **Store Visits:** This provides the number of people who have visited your store or stores after seeing your ads on Facebook.

IV. *Scheduling and Sharing Reports*

The following list will help you to understand the various actions available in the Reports section of the Facebook Ads Manager.

- **Schedule:** You can schedule reports to send automatically to anyone that has access to the account. This can be done on a daily, weekly, or even monthly basis, and you can maintain as many as a thousand reports in your ad account.

- **Export:** You can also export reports or advertising data directly into Microsoft Excel, using the free Excel Add-on available in Facebook Ads Manager.

- **Share:** If you do not to send or export the reports, you can also create a clickable link to the Ad Manager and you can share that link.

- **Download:** Finally, you can download reports as .csv or .xls files. These reports can then be copied to a USB drive, attached to an email, sent via instant messenger, or shared in any other way possible.

In addition, the Microsoft Office Store offers a plugin with Facebook Ads Manager, which allows you to download ad account directly into Excel. With this plug-in, you can:

- Download performance data using reporting controls - like filters - so that you can create custom reports in Ads Manager.
- Create custom templates that allow you to run reports quickly.
- Refresh the data as often as necessary.
- Use Excel's pivot tables and other tools to generate a custom analysis of ad performance.

The Excel plug-in is just as user-friendly and customizable as the Facebook Ad Manager, allowing you to create report templates that are based entirely on the metrics most important to you and your business.

Chapter 5: What Will It Cost? – Effective Budgeting For Your Facebook Campaign

I. Budget

Creating and maintaining a budget with Facebook Ads Manager is easy. You can tailor every aspect of the ad campaign to fit within your budget, and the Ads Manager will quickly let know if your budget is too small for your goals.

Facebook Ads Manager refers to your budget as an "Auction." The Auction determines which ads are shown to which audiences, based on the demographics you choose. The ad is always shown to the audience that is most likely to be interested, and once the price (or bid) is set, Facebook Ads Manager will never show your ad in a way that might exceed your bid, or what you are willing to spend on the campaign in question.

During the ad creation process, you will set specific parameters, including:

- **Budget:** This is the total amount you are willing to spend over the course of the campaign - whether the campaign is scheduled to last one day, one month or longer. You can edit your budget at any time, but you will be asked to set a maximum amount that Facebook Ads Manager will never exceed without your express permission.
- **Audience:** This tool allows you to choose who sees your ad campaign. Your audience can be tailored depending on age, gender, or location.

- **Creative:** This tool allows you to choose how your ad appears - whether you use text, images or videos to capture the attention of your target audience.

Facebook Ads Manager also provides two specialty buying options, Reach & Frequency and Target Rating Points.

- **Reach & Frequency:** This specialty buying option is ideal if your campaign needs to target more than 200,000 people. It provides controlled ad delivery at a locked price. For more information, visit the Facebook Business page at: https://www.facebook.com/business/learn/facebook-reach-and-frequency-buying
- **Target Rating Points:** This specialty buying option allows you to purchase video ads on Facebook, much like you would if you were purchasing television ads on a national network. For more information, visit the Facebook Business FAQ page at https://www.facebook.com/business/help/518993728299293

Facebook ad campaigns can cost you as little as $5.00 a week, or as much as $50,000 a week. This aspect is highly customizable. Once a budget is set, Facebook Ad Manager will automatically calculate the "audience reach," based on your budget and the length of time you have chosen to run the campaign. If you want your ad to reach a wider audience, you can either increase your budget or reduce the length of your ad campaign.

The Ads Manager will also calculate the cost per result for you. If you, or your client, want to set a budget based on the cost per result (instead of a budget based on the campaign as a whole), this calculation is the one you will need to look at most closely.

In addition, Facebook Ads Manager allows to tailor your budget even further in the following ways:

- Campaign Spending Limit: This parameter allows you to set the maximum amount you are willing to spend on the advertising campaign in question. This is your overall budget for a SINGLE ad.
- Account Spending Limit: This parameter allows you to set a maximum amount you are willing to spend on ALL of your campaigns, not just one particular ad.

Given the specific requirements of your advertising campaign, like the budget, bid, or targeted audience, the Ads Manager will give you an estimate how many people your advertisement will reach before you actually publish the ad. This is especially useful if you or your client are unsure about your budget or audience.

Once your ad campaign has been published, you will receive performance updates throughout the campaign. These results are available on the "Insights" tab in the Ads Manager. It is very important to take these updates into consideration throughout the campaign, as adjustments to the campaign parameters may be necessary to hit your performance goals - like increasing your budget, or reducing or expanding your audience.

If, for some reason, your ad campaign is completely unsuccessful, and Facebook Ads Manager is unable to obtain the results that were quoted to you when the ad was published - whether the issue is related to your budget or your ad strategy - Facebook Ads Manager will stop delivering the ad and you will not be charged if you did not receive results. This "guarantee" is especially important for first-time advertisers and small business owners that have a tight advertising budget.

II. Delivering Ad Campaigns

Facebook Ads Manager goes to great lengths to ensure that your ad campaign is only seen by an audience interested in what you are advertising. This prevents audience members from issuing complaints about advertisements that are not relevant to them, and it prevents you from spending your advertising budget in a manner that is not beneficial to your business or brand.

The goal of the Facebook Ads Manager is to make sure that the right ad is seen by the right audience at the right time. This is different from traditional advertising, which is focused more on the "value" of an ad. Traditionally, several ad agencies will create a campaign based on your proposal, and would then submit bids in an effort to obtain the contract. Those campaigns are then evaluated from a monetary standpoint; typically, the cheapest campaign would be chosen.

With Facebook Ads Manager, you can obtain the results you want on almost any budget - as you are in complete control of the parameters you set for your campaign. Even if someone else sets a higher ad budget, your ad may still reach more audience members or have better overall performance. It is entirely up to you, and with Facebook Ads Manager, you have every tool you need to guarantee success in your ad campaign.

III. Ad Auctions

A Facebook Ad Auction determines which advertisements are shown to which customers or users, based on the information provided during the ad creation process and the structuring of the ad campaign. The Auction ensures that your ad is shown to customers or users who are "most likely" to be interested in your business, product, or brand - and it makes sure that your ad is never shown to those customers at a higher price than was agreed upon in your budget.

Facebook Ad Auctions use the following parameters to determine which ad is seen by which user:

- *Budget:* At this point, you will have already set a budget for your ad campaign - both your daily budget and your "ad lifetime" budget.
- *Audience:* At this point, you will have chosen your audience by age, gender, location and more.
- *Creative:* This refers to your ad design - whether it is an image, a video, text only, a slideshow, et cetera.

In addition to those parameters, Facebook Ad Auctions also offer two unique "ad buying options."

- *Reach & Frequency:* This option is ideal if you want your ad to reach more than 200,000 people. It gives you a predictable ad cycle on a set budget.
- *Target Rating Points:* For those accustomed to purchasing television ads, this is very similar. You can use this option if you are interested in purchasing video ads.

Facebook Ad Auctions always run within the budget you set when you designed your ad campaign. You can spend as little as $5 per week or as much $50,000 per week. The cost of your campaign is broken down into these categories:

- *Campaign Spending Limit:* this is the maximum amount you are willing to spend on the entire ad campaign.
- *Account Spending Limit:* this is the maximum amount you are will to spend on every ad campaign on your account.

Using these two limits, and the parameters provided when you designed your ad campaign, Facebook Ads Manager will then provide you with an estimate of how many people or customers they expect your ad to reach - all before you actually publish your ad! This will allow you to think, yet again, about your ad budget and whether or not you need to increase it. Remember - Facebook Ads Manager will *never* exceed the budget you set.

Facebook Ad Auctions also seek to make sure that you always achieve the results you expect to achieve while making sure that the customers never see ads that are not relevant to them. This keeps both parties happy and provides a positive experience for all involved.

When a Facebook Ad Auction takes place, Facebook uses the information provided in a customer's profile to match them with several different ads. The ad that is ultimately displayed for that customer is the ad that will cost the *least* amount to display. This guarantees that the ad marketplace is fair and unbiased and that advertising accounts never receive preference or special treatment. The decision is based entirely on the budget of the ad campaign and whether or not the ad is suitable for the customer in question.

Each time your ad is displayed, Facebook Ads Manager will then use part of your previously determined budget to pay for that ad. Facebook Ads Manager will always use the smallest amount of your budget funds possible. This means you will frequently be charged less than you anticipated, and you will rarely need to increase your budget to achieve your original goals. You should only ever need to increase your budget if you have determined that your ad campaign is more successful than expected - and therefore you decide to run the campaign for a longer period of time than originally planned.

Conclusion

Thank for making it through to the end of *Facebook Marketing & Advertising: The Ultimate Guide for Beginners and Startups*! We hope it was informative and that it has provided you with all of the tools you need to achieve your goals with social media marketing on the Facebook platform.

Remember:

- Respect copyright laws! Make sure your ad content is either completely original, or that you have obtained the necessary copyright releases for the images, videos, or other content you may be using.
- Utilize the reports available within the Facebook Ads Manager! With these reports, you can learn exactly how to create and manage a successful and profitable ad campaign, time and time again.
- Choose your audience carefully! A narrow audience may be ideal for strictly targeted ad campaigns, but a broad audience may be better if you are looking to increase overall profits or website traffic.
- Your budget is not set in stone! Facebook Ads Manager makes it incredibly easy to tailor your budget to your needs, without ever going over-budget. You can add money at any time, and Facebook will only ever bill you on a month-to-month basis - never charging for what has not been used in the campaign.

Finally, we would greatly appreciate your feedback in the form of an Amazon review, especially if you found this guide to be informative and helpful.

www.ingramcontent.com/pod-product-compliance
Lightning Source LLC
Chambersburg PA
CBHW030100230526
45471CB00003B/1185